D0817444

Intruders, **HALT!** You are in the king's forest! State your business!

Our business is evil!

EVIL!

We will storm the castle and eat the queen!

I am a **WICKED WIZARD** whose magic amulet will bring eternal darkness to the land!

I am the wizard's **EVIL OWL** who doesn't like the sun, anyways!

6

But where others saw tragedy, the great Otto Airs saw an opportunity!

My new movie will be the crowning of the next king!

I will combine film and reality T.V. and make it in 3D.

It will be a triumph!

But what happened to the real king?

I've already made a casting call for the movie!

That must be all those people mobbing the castle.

Everyone wants to be in my movie.

Can I be in your movie... PLEASE?

You really have no idea how this business works, do you?

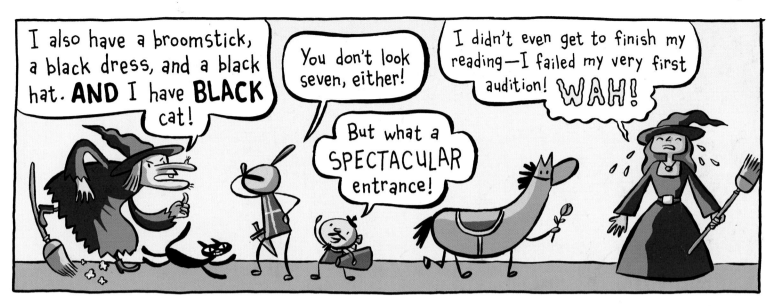

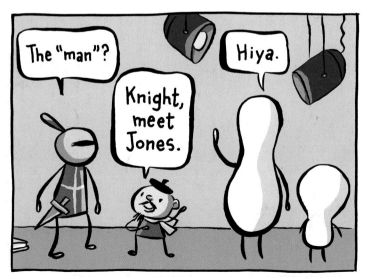

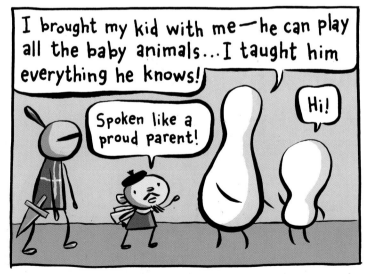

I've created all kinds of creatures, like the **COCK-A-DOODLE CHEESE DOODLE!**

The **PEANUT BUTTER AND JELLY FISH!**

The BOAT-A-SAURUS!

The CLOWN-A-CLOPS!

Now, for my next creation, I will combine a ballerina and a piece of broccoli!

Edward, NO!

RIGHT! It's called **BODY LANGUAGE!** Can you tell the difference between the beggar and the knight?

I sure can!!!

I could also tell them apart from their clothes.

Excellent Point!

Your sword and helmet tell me you are a knight, but now...

You changed me into a PIRATE!

And a COWGIRL BANDIT! YEE-HAW!!!

NOW I'M A **DEEP-SEA DIVER!!!**

The right costume can change any character!

Get a load of all the wizards!

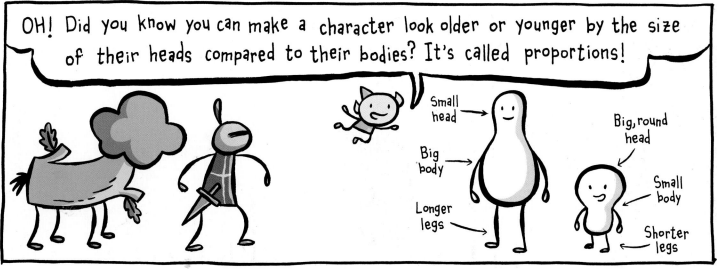

OH! Did you know you can make a character look older or younger by the size of their heads compared to their bodies? It's called proportions!

Small head

Big body

Longer legs

Big, round head

Small body

Shorter legs

ABOUT THE AUTHORS

Alexis loves helping in the garden.

They say the author is a three-headed cartooning monster, but I don't believe in monsters.

Me neither.

ANDREW ARNOLD HAS A ROBOTIC ARM.

James stole my boots, and I want them back.

Cartoonists are shy so they use hand puppets to talk to people they don't know.

Andrew is my favorite.

The little piggy who stayed home is every cartoonist's favorite.

I really can't remember anything about the authors.

Betcha the authors of this book can't do this! NO HANDS!!!

The authors of this book are the kindest, most talented people I have ever met in my entire life.

Now can I have that cookie you promised me?

First Second

New York

Copyright © 2013 by James Sturm, Andrew Arnold, and Alexis Frederick-Frost

Published by First Second
First Second is an imprint of Roaring Brook Press, a division of Holtzbrinck Publishing Holdings Limited Partnership
175 Fifth Avenue, New York, New York 10010

All rights reserved

Cataloging-in-Publication Data is on file at the Library of Congress

ISBN: 978-1-59643-732-6

First Second books are available for special promotions and premiums.
For details, contact: Director of Special Markets, Holtzbrinck Publishers.

First edition
2013
Printed in China by Macmillan Production (Asia) Ltd., Kowloon Bay, Hong Kong (supplier code 10)

10 9 8 7 6 5 4 3 2 1

NEW FEATURE: THE MIGHTY AIC BOOKS ASSEMBLE!

It's so BORING in this dungeon!

NOT FOR LONG!

WHAT'S THIS?! Are you here to help me escape?!

We're the ADVENTURES IN CARTOONING books!

WE'LL SAVE THE DAY!!!

I radiate CREATIVE energy!

I generate HOLIDAY spirit!

Grab a pencil! I'm INTERACTIVE!

How will that help me escape?!

We're RESCUING you from boredom!

ESCAPE INTO YOUR IMAGINATION!

Meanwhile, inside Edward's indestructible stomach...

THE END. (again!)